I ♥ MY ROOM

Children's rooms you and your children will love...

I ♥ MY ROOM

made by megan morton, jason busch and penny shek

CONTENTS

LIVING WITH KIDS

By Megan Morton

Kids and their bedrooms are definitely at odds with each other. This is why I chose to make a book that dealt with the challenges and charm of kids' spaces — mostly from the front line. With virtually no pre-styling to speak of, (yes, some kids really are just neat) these rooms are all inspiring, but very much the rooms of real kids.

Now, some people's version of 'tidy' is different to others' and it is the real perspectives that can be found through these pages. From whimsical nurseries to expressive teen spaces, we want to leave you giddy with excitement for your own brood's room. Take inspiration from Sunday and Roman's pea-green bunk room or Luca's Smurf-swamped tele, the whispering softness of almost-lilac in Jemima's room (by the way, it is Dulux Fog Bay) and Ella and Marley's adventurously spirited haven.

As a mother to three magical kids, I also wanted to address some of the more nuts-and-bolts specifics of setting up a kid's room. What makes these kids' rooms so successful is that it has usually been the kids themselves have inspired the spaces. Acknowledging what sort of child you have on your hands is a big step in getting it right. And believe me, it's not even a family genetic one-size-fits-all-rule; each child will operate differently, no matter how close in age. I am in no way an authority on children's rooms, but having my own children over a very large age gap (14 down to 3), I know all too well the challenges that the family home faces. While I have broken it down into age groups so it's more digestible (we all know that a mother of twin four year olds won't have a millisecond spare to read past her own age group) there are general tips littered throughout that may prove to be your breakthrough point.

In my travels I have also come to realise that no matter how large the room is (or isn't), if it's being done with small change or on an allocated budget, we are all faced with the same issues. But whatever way you play it, don't be a hypocrite and impose double (bedroom) standards.

Oh and...

1. If they are past the age of six, don't throw their things out after having three coffees during the school holidays. It's really unfair.

2. When you ask them what kind of room they want and they answer 'purple' they don't necessarily mean it. They have never renovated, developed their style or designed a room. Not only will they want you to paint all four walls purple, they will expect you to 'interpret' the purple they like, but don't feel obliged and don't forget who's the boss!

Newborns and Nurseries.

Nurseries are totally up for debate. I produced some dud rooms for my first two children and our dear wee baby lives happily (for the time being) in our room. Not because we couldn't manage a room for her, but because we really wanted her in with us, for all the reasons we wanted the first two out!

Position the cot or bed away from the natural light source, or install a block-out blind. Once baby is down it should be shut-eye time.

Plan on rompers, onsies and baby tracksuits to be their at-home staples. A lot of the time we iron beautiful linen, cotton dresses and shirts only to find that they have outgrown them before the occasion arises. Sadly the whole wardrobe can become redundant and open-topped storage boxes that offer easy access become your primary go-to dressing source. Given the amount of washing you do, it is easier to dry, fold and dump than hang up in a robe.

Don't make up for your own lost childhood bedroom dreams like I did. Growing up on a banana farm in very undecorated surrounds, my firstborn's room was a shrine to poppies and totally over coordinated. No wonder my baby hated sleeping in there. I would too. I mean, who needs to have six matching pillows to negotiate with before going to sleep? And yes, I also did a wall frieze — this is my biggest shame.

Consider a finial secured to a wall as a safer alternative to a loose doorstop. This will also reduce risk of jammed fingers when doors fling open and slam close.

Don't be too fussed on allocating the quietest room in the house to the baby. You want to have a baby that is a good sleeper; one that can sleep through usual levels of noise. Sometimes insisting on silence breeds an inflexible mind when it comes to sleeping in other situations, which is a pain when you are at someone's house past bedtime or away on holidays.

While it is hard to envisage a life after the first couple of sleepless years, consider what sort of family life you want to roll with. Are you hoping to be fairly loose or does it suit you and yours to run things like clockwork? Trying to imagine life when they are six can help you make formative decisions. Because how you start off will inform where you will finish.

Not Babies Anymore.

Consider placing hooks (or another hanging rod) halfway down the robe wall so they can reach it and could potentially hang up clothes themselves. Kids' sized hangers will also help.

If the room is pushed for space, consider removing cupboard or wardrobe doors (that aren't on space-saving sliders) and replacing them with curtains. Softening any room, the hanging curtain gives great access, conceals mess and lets the room gain real, as well as perceived, space.

Make self bed-making easy (if that is how you want it to roll) and don't expect it to be to the standard you like. Agree on what is acceptable, set the bar and leave them to do it. Unless you like spending half an hour making everyone's beds.

At the moment, every artwork is precious. But believe me, you will amass thousands of pieces before they get to their times tables. A rope with pegs (or pin board) allows you to showcase the newcomers and select some for keepsake.

I don't encourage chalkboards in kids' rooms. Sure, it can look cute to have their markings up, but I did my son's entire room in it, (page 46) and I came to detest the chalk dust and the maintenance required to keep it looking A-1.

Toys can pile up into truly embarrassing amounts. You will find it difficult to believe and look at them all and wonder, 'Wow, how could we afford to buy all of this?' The embarrassment wanes when you pass toys on to St Vinnies or circulate them between friends and relatives. (Or better still, you can register with a toy club in your area and high five yourself for being so efficient). Even if you only have a small amount of toys compared to others you know, put them into boxes and rotate the feature toys every couple of months. I actually label and date mine so I can keep her boredom at bay and fool her into thinking she has a Toy-Tree in the top cupboard!

Teenagers.

I once interviewed the super clever Nest Architects who shared great insight into kids' rooms. The principle architect, Emilio, commented that you shouldn't make their rooms too big, or spaces they 'can get lost in', as the whole idea is to push them out of there and to encourage them to spend time in shared spaces.

At this age they may want to be involved in a conversation about room dressing and styling. So if they are keen on a colour or theme, try and be willing to go there — within reason, of course. Encouraging this can mean a lot to their visual independence. My poor parents, who were decoratively void, had to put up with me creating mini collages under contact to make 'limited edition light switch plates'!

Did you hang up all your clothes when you where a school kid? Answer honestly. You may have blessed your own with a diligent neat gene, lucky you. If not, try not to be a total stickler on this point. My son has plenty of hanging space but nothing hanging — most falls to the bottom of the wardrobe floor. So instead of riding him on it, I placed a series of hooks right near his door. Once school is done for the week, I hang (clean) options on the hooks (along with any corresponding bags with gear and equipment) that he might need during the course of the busy weekend. This way he has all occasions covered, as well as possible weather contingency options.

Provide them with their own dirty washing bins. Expecting them to walk to the laundry or even the shoot is possibly unrealistic. A lidded one is best, given a busy week can really change the atmosphere of the room if left uncovered!

Sometimes even opening and closing a drawer can be difficult for a teen. No matter how many drawers you provide for folded clothes and smalls, sometimes those wire plastic coated shelves mounted to the inside of the robe door are more effective. One can be for socks, another for underwear and so on.

If you're building new, consider more electrical points in this room, or provide access to multiple points. Teens are likely to be charging many electronic devices and if provided, it will save them from using or moving yours. And a side note, I insist a book for every electronic game, video or DVD. Appreciating the written word is important and at risk at being lost with this generation of kids.

This is also the age group that needs very clear and efficient lighting for study and reading. Place small cup hooks to the inside legs of bedside tables and desks that can hold the loose cords of phone, laptops or computers.

Oh, and a full-length mirror on the back of the door so they can check themselves out before leaving the house.

When it comes to sporting, school and hobby achievements, you may be gushing with pride and want to keep the proof visible, but the self-conscious teen will probably prefer to banish such to the cupboard. I have seen a compromise on this with a small narrow shelf that sits above the bedroom door holding prized trophies, the infrequently handled memorabilia or the dreaded family framed photo! This position keeps them out of harm's (or a basketball's) way, isn't embarrassing and usually goes undetected by visitors and friends.

And if it's really an unmanageable scene, not to worry, just leave the window open for circulation, buy them good quality headphones and keep the door closed!

Betty Jean

& Evie

A family that makes together sticks together! All three of the Wolkenstein girls are a force. Mother and teacher Rebecca and her daughters Betty Jean and Evie call the beautiful Southern Highlands home. Here they share the bounty of their chickens, vegetable garden, self-taught macramé and homemade face masks with husband and father, photographer Julian Wolkenstein.

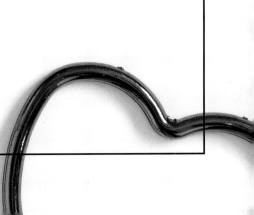

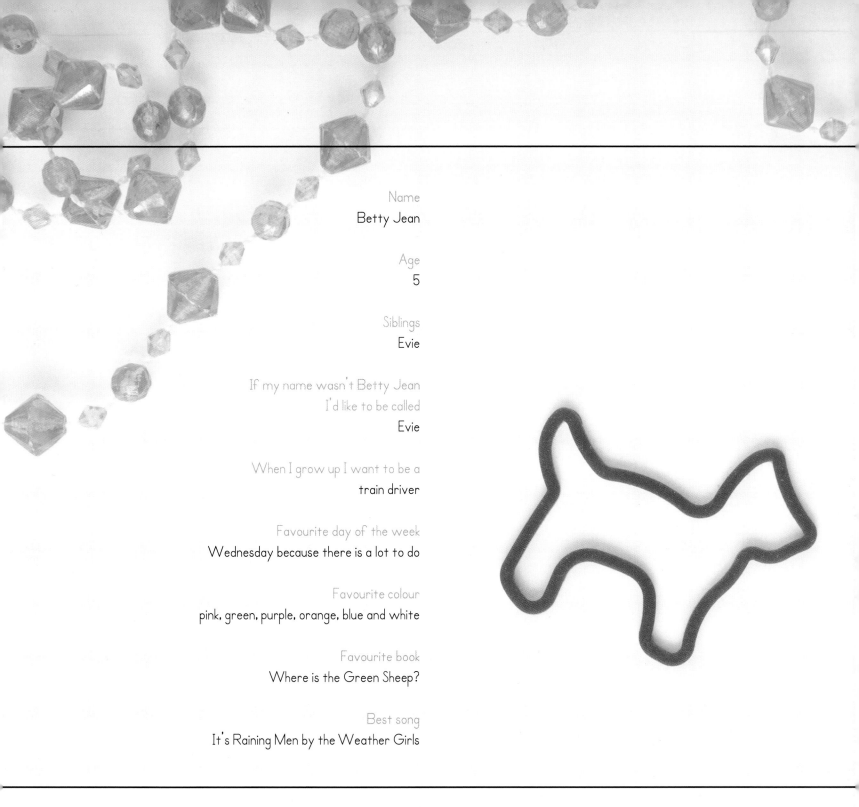

Name
Betty Jean

Age
5

Siblings
Evie

If my name wasn't Betty Jean
I'd like to be called
Evie

When I grow up I want to be a
train driver

Favourite day of the week
Wednesday because there is a lot to do

Favourite colour
pink, green, purple, orange, blue and white

Favourite book
Where is the Green Sheep?

Best song
It's Raining Men by the Weather Girls

Name
Evie (Guinevere)

Age
3 1/2

My mum and dad are
Rebecca and Julian

If my name wasn't Evie I'd like to be called
Betty

When I grow up I want to be a
train driver

Best friends
Spencer, Paddy, Betty and Mim

Favourite day of the week
Sunday

Favourite colour
red

Favourite book
Sophie's Big Bed

Best song
I Can Sing a Rainbow

Best thing about my room
toys

What do you sleep with at night?
hot water bottle

BRIDGETTE

Maybe her room does have a head start with her mother, Tina, being one of the more daring interior designers in Sydney. Bridgette de Salis sleeps and plays by the lilac polka dots of her revamped wardrobe (found at a flea market) and her wall-mounted bird house. The upholstered bedhead and lounge Tina made has a Cinderella flair. "It is all so soft," says Bridgette of her room, "so soft and squidgy!"

Name
Bridgette

Age
4

My mum and dad are
Tina and Ed

Where in the family
first born

If my name wasn't Bridgette
I'd like to be called
Wendy (from Peter Pan)

Favourite colour
pink and red

When I grow up I want to be a
ballet teacher, an actor or a fixer

Favourite book
Peter Pan

Favourite movie
Wizard of Oz

My teddy is called
Pogo

B : "My favourite toy is Ariel Barbie."

LUCA

Luca's papa is an architect, a well-revered one. However, his room shows zero sign of this with a permanent train track laid on the floor and a black, plastic car bed. According to Luca, the best thing in his room would have to be his tele in the playroom. Fully loaded with Smurf figurines, it is no wonder Luca's place is a popular play-date destination.

Name
Luca

Age
6

My mum and dad are
Lisa and Stephen

If my name wasn't Luca I'd like to be called
Sam

When I grow up I want to be an
artist

Best friends
Jake and Sammy

Favourite book
Dr Seuss

Favourite colour
gold

Best song
Beat It by Michael Jackson

Favourite movie
Wizards of Waverly Place

Elodie

It is the kind of room that little girls' dreams are made of. Soft timber, white with pastel highlights, Elodie's room is pretty, no doubt about it, but more than that it is practical. Minimally dressed is what makes its pretty elements stand out. This space proves that sometimes a room needs the bare necessities, played out in soft colours with zero conflict.

Name
Elodie

Age
4

If my name wasn't Elodie I'd like to be called
Max

When I grow up I want to be a
crocodile feeder

Best friends
Minty, Sadie, Camille and Meaniac (my teddy bear)

Favourite day of the week
treat day, which is Friday

Favourite colour
pink and green and yellow

Favourite book
Hello Kitty

Best song
I Like it Like That by Guy Sebastian

Best thing about my room
the stickers on my bed

E : "My favourite movie is Ponyo."

Yasmin & Harper

Living in the Big Apple in smaller spaces means brother and sister Harper Cloudy and Yasmin Tallulah have to be clever in their approach. Mandatory clean-ups every school holidays help these little rooms work at their maximum. Harper's can sleep three with his genius plywood bunk and Yas's white space allows her love of teal, her guitar and small rubbers to shine.

Name **Yasmin**

My mum and dad are
Vanessa and Simon

Age
11

Siblings
Harper

If my name wasn't Yasmin I'd like to be called
Alice or Holly

Favourite colour
blue

Best song
Pearl by Katy Perry

Favourite movie
Kiki's Delivery Service

Favourite book
too many to list — reading is my favourite thing to do

Y ⚇ "When I grow up I want to be a pet shop owner."

Name
Harper

Age
9

If my name wasn't Harper I'd like to be called
Tintin

When I grow up I want to be a
candy shop owner with my own candy

Best friends
Noah, Jackson, Isabella, Kamryn and Baz

Favourite day of the week
Friday

Favourite colour
blue

Favourite book
How to Grow Up and Rule the World
by Vordak the Incomprehensible

Best song
Living on a Prayer by Bon Jovi

Favourite toy
My Nintendo DS

Favourite movie
Scott Pilgrim vs. the World

H : **"The best thing about my room is I have two beds."**

Millie & Sebastian.

Adamant that they wanted a room of their own, these siblings specifically requested to remove the door in between for "late night chats and all things secret". Sebastian's has been painted chalkboard black while Millie's is left to host a growing amount of mixed-media artwork, including her own. Room opening and dividing doesn't require two rooms, something like a back-to-back wardrobe can make a new division to create a semi-private scenario. Don't let size dictate a potential division, as these spaces show sometimes all that is needed is room for a bed and robe.

Name
Sebastian

Age
9

Where in the family
piggy in the middle

When I grow up I want to be a
mechanical engineer

Best friends
Fergus

Favourite colour
black

Favourite toy
a tool kit

Best song
Shine by Vanessa Amorosi

Best thing about my room
my comfy bed

My teddy is called
Jon Lilis

What do you sleep with at night?
my blanket

What's your favourite movie?

s: I am a movie freak and I can't
      narrow it down to one

Name
Millicent

My mum and dad are
Megan (stylist) and Giles (fast runner)

Age
10

When I grow up I want to be a
vet

Favourite day of the week
Fridays!

Favourite colour
pink (light pink)

Favourite book
Black Beauty

Favourite toy
my computer

What do you sleep with at night?
my dog August

Jemima

Jemima's mum places fresh flowers on her mantelpiece. It is this genetic predisposition that has Jemima loving all things pretty. Her charming, big iron bed allows room for sleepovers and despite its size she has managed to squeeze in plenty of art supplies and storage around it. She utilises all available space, with the non-working fireplace a home for her books. Doused in lilac and dusty pinks, the room plays it visually 'light', allowing for her artwork and craft to pop.

Name
Jemima

My mum and dad are
Daniel and Heidi

Age
6

When I grow up I want to be a
zoo keeper

What's your favourite day of the week?
every day

Favourite colour
blue

Favourite book
pop—up books

Best song
ABBA

Best thing about my room
toys

Favourite movie
Monsters vs Aliens

My teddy is called
Lara

Who is your best friend?

J: my WHOLE KLUS

tyke and ari

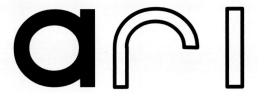
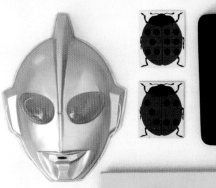

In this case sharing a room is both by choice and need. For Ari and Tyke it is double the fun. Talented designer Beci Orpin's boys' room is chockers with wooden toys, games and kitsch reminders of her own idyllic, hippy childhood. Their Papa, Raph Rashid, food-truck entrepreneur and owner of Melbourne's much-loved Beatbox Kitchen and Taco Truck ensures they all have great food, good times and great music while their bunk beds make for sound sleeps.

Name
Tyke

Age
8

When I grow up I want to be a
skateboarder

Best friends
Matthew, Umut, Ben, Jay and Milo

Favourite book
Zac Power

Best song
More by Usher

Best thing about my room
loft bed

Favourite movie
Star Wars

Name
Ari

Age
4

My mum and dad are
mama (Beci) and pups (Raph)

Siblings
big bro, Tyke

If my name wasn't Ari I'd like to be called
Harry Potter

When I grow up I want to be
Bear Grylls

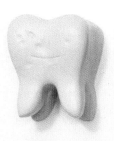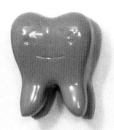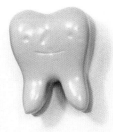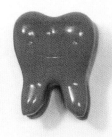

Favourite book
The Dangerous Journey

Best thing about my room
sharing with my brother

Best song
Girlfriend by Best Coast

Favourite toy
mama's iPhone

e friends went and Bella
ent to sleep dreaming hap

eams   the
uppy   ing

ella
arents   Before

he d   aid

honey   has

tone   what"

said Bella my puppy has

tone missing

Name
Eva

My mum and dad are
Susan and Michael

Age
9

Siblings
Milly and Henry

Where in the family
youngest

If my name wasn't Eva I'd like to be called
Isabel

Best friends
May, Julia, Charlotte and Alannah

Favourite colour
yellow

Favourite book
Jane Blonde

Best song
Someday by the Black Eyed Peas

Favourite movie
Flipped

eva

At age 9, Eva has lived in New York and London,
but her Sydney bedroom is her favourite.

e: "the best thing about my room is...

it's big!"

Lana and Scarlet

Proving that both chaos and order can reign, Lana and Scarlet's rooms pay homage to knockout colours and collections that are anything but juvenile. How is a room like this managed? Creatively by their parents—Liane Rossler, one of the founders of Dinosaur Designs, and Sam Marshall, architect. The planning and storage designed by Sam and the collision of clutter by Liane results in rooms that have every surface covered. The clever magnetic and pin-board walls make sure every piece of artwork generated by the girls has a home.

Name
Lana

Age
10

My mum and dad are
Liane and Sam

If my name wasn't Lana I'd like to be called
Hazel

When I grow up I want to be a
pre-school teacher

Best friends
Alba, Hila and Estelle

Favourite book
A Series of Unfortunate Events

Best song
Who Says by Selena Gomez

Favourite movie
Ramona and Beezus

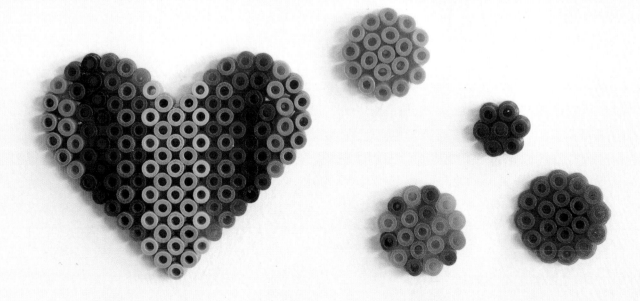

Name
Scarlet

Age
7

If my name wasn't Scarlet
I'd like to be called
Pearl

Best friends
Billie, Lilly and Jazmyn

Favourite colour
aqua

Favourite book
Gerald McBoing Boing, One Blue Sock
and Queen Munch and Queen Nibble

Best song
Mine by Taylor Swift and lullabies

Favourite toy
Ladybug (bear) and Rabbie (rabbit)

Favourite movie
Valentine's Day

Best thing about my room is
posters, bedside table, bed and toys

What do you sleep with at night?
Ladybug, Moo Moo, Sea Sea, Silver Bell and Teddy

ELLa AND

marLey

Megan Park's textiles and children's clothes can be bold and can be sweet. While her home undergoes a room-by-room renovation, her twin's shared room has been given a soft, decorative makeover in a neutral palette. Flexible beds and an antique armoire are the only things not made from fabric. Wall murals, toys and bunting mostly made by Indian artisans fill the small space. While it will eventually become cramped as the twins grow, for now it is the perfect space for them.

E: "The best thing about my room is... my Indian picture."

Name	Name
Marley Ray	Ella May
Age	Age
3	3
When I grow up I want to be a	When I grow up I want to be a
fireman	pink princess
If my name wasn't Marley	If my name wasn't Ella
I'd like to be called	I'd like to be called
Scary Dragon	Pink Princess
Best Friends	Best Friends
Leo Buckle	Sunday, Marley, Charlie, Scout, Lucy, Hannah, Pepa, Hazel
and Walter	and Walter
Favourite book	Favourite book
Slinky Malinky	Pinkalicious
Best song	Best song
Five Little Ducks	Watermelon
Favourite toy	Favourite toy
my big digger	my bus
Favourite movie	Favourite movie
Toy Story	red shoes (Wizard of Oz)

APRIL

April is the queen of dressing up—she has so many head pieces that she barely has enough time to wear them! With a mum who is a star sewer, April's many costume changes can be easily accommodated. Her room is pretty simply styled, with her dressing room and playground adding colour and character.

A: "WHEN I GROW UP I WANT TO BE A PRINCESS."

Name
April

My mum and dad are
Louise and Martin

Age
5

Best friends
Amelia, Greta and Charlotte

Favourite day of the week
Friday fun night! tv and staying up late

Favourite colour
pink

Favourite book
Pippi Longstocking

Best song
Over the Rainbow

Favourite movie
Sound of Music and Enchanted

Best thing about my room
my bed

JULES

Smart! What smarts! Why track down rolls and rolls of vintage wallpaper for the one room when you can make a tapestry from mixed rolls? Jules' room is a mixed bag of eras and genres sourced by his ever-crafty mum. A smattering of kitsch and vintage pieces are applied practically.

Name
Jules

Age
8

If my name wasn't Jules
I'd like to be called
Richard or Zac

When I grow up I want to be a
chef, builder or drummer

Best friends
Luka, Sage and Tim

Favourite book
The BFG by Roald Dahl

Favourite toy
lego

Favourite movie
Home Alone

Best thing about my room is
big bed and big room

Maddie

There are five Percy children, and if we had space, we would show all of their rooms! Each room shows individual flair and their discrepancy in age. This is Maddie's (the eldest). Remember teenagers do love a knick knack. It is best to provide a place for them to show off their talismans, trophies and bits and bobs. Wall-mounted storage boxes can be handy—things are better up off the floor than on it! It becomes their own teen mantlepiece, a place to put the things that matter most to them.

Name
Maddie

Age
13

My mum and dad are
cool but strict

If my name wasn't Maddie I'd like to be called
Stella

Where in the family
top of the food chain

When I grow up I want to be a
fashion designer or actress / singer

Best friends
Tals, Audrey, Zara, Lucy, Mina and Ursula

Favourite book
Dash and Lily's Book of Dares

Best song
Sparks Fly by Taylor Swift

Favourite toy
my polaroid camera

Best thing about my room
my chocolate freckle rug

Nicholas & Sasha

Sasha wants to be an artist and Nicholas wants to own a gallery. Their rooms speak volumes about their personal preferences and take over the first floor of their family home. The strategy—run by their mother—is all about small works of art that will kickstart a collection that can be added to over a lifetime. Smaller works can then grow and over time will amass! Channel your inner galleriest—start a collection and watch it grow!

Name
Sasha

Age
11

Where in the family
oldest + coolest!

When I grow up I want to be a
artist or chef

Best friends
lots, too many to write!

Favourite day of the week
Saturday

Favourite colour
rainbow

Best song
Price Tag by Jessie J ♡

Favourite toy
Peppy

Best thing about my room
my bunnies

N: "The best thing about my room is my bed!"

Name
Nick

My mum and dad are
funny

Age
9

When I grow up I want to be an
Olympic sailor

Favourite day of the week
Friday (of course)

Favourite book
Holes by Louis Sachar

Best song
Joker and the Thief by Wolfmother

Favourite movie
Morning Light,
because it is a sailing movie

willow

Willow's parents own a caravan, a really cute one.
She picnics and plays in secluded beachside spots—it's
the kind of life most people fantasise about. Lucky Willow.
When she is home, a black nursery and a hanging Noah's
basket are her base, but she is soothed by the movement
of the car come the weekends.

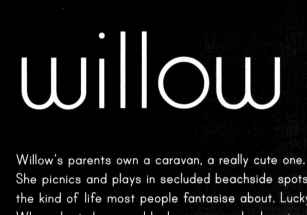

Hello! My name is Willow. I am baby and I live in Melbourne with my mum and dad and my four legged, furry brother Grover (he is old and a little bit grumpy). My mum and dad have a fashion label called Elk. Grover and I go to work with them most days where they have set up a very comfortable nursery for me. I am really lucky because the staff at the studio love to give me cuddles. On the weekends we go to our caravan on the beach where I love to go for walks with my dad. My favourite thing to do is to watch for birds, although most of the time I fall asleep. —W

Indigo & Chilli

Art lovers and furniture designers, Mark and Louella Tuckey's daughters' rooms have not one square inch of wall space left. A low-line, wooden bed means the rooms present larger and allow space for more art to fill the walls. Deliberately doused in soft woods and neutral linens, the artwork boasts bold colour, making it an engaging place to retreat to. Toys are stored in their rooms and there is not a hint of plastic insight.

Name
Indigo

Age
3

When I grow up I want to be a
schoolgirl

Favourite book
Puff the Magic Dragon

What do you sleep with at night?
Ra Ra

RaRa →

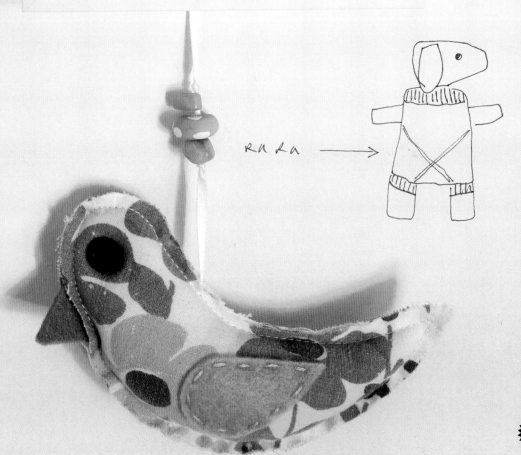

Name
Chilli

Age
5

When I grow up I want to be a
ballerina

Favourite book
Angelina Ballerina

Best song
Love Story by Taylor Swift

Favourite day of the week
Monday

Favourite colour
pink, purple, violet, and rainbow

Favourite movie
Spirit

What do you sleep with at night?
twins

twins

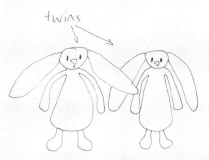

CHARLIE AND COCO

Charlie and Coco speak French to their mother Cecile and probably don't realise how French their rooms are. Mostly decked out in furniture sourced at the flea markets of France, Cecile has chosen pieces that won't need to be updated in the near future. Charlie has a double bed and flag regalia while Coco's metal bed and wooden armoire will be used well into her teens. Cecile owns a French boutique called Bonjour, and it is in these rooms where items are tried and tested under the practical hands of her own children before deemed suitable for her store. Cecile aims for decor that is both beautiful and practical and in Charlie and Coco's rooms she has achieved both.

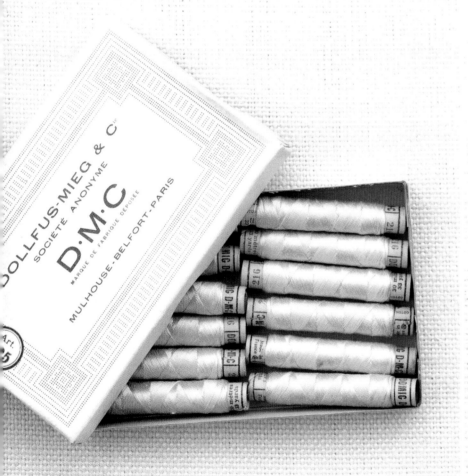

Name
Coco

My mum and dad are
Cecile and Guy

Age
3

If my name wasn't Coco
I'd like to be called
Cecile Maman

Where in the family
the little one

Best friends
Claudine, Marine and Eden

Favourite colour
pink

Favourite book
Three Little Pigs

Favourite toy
my doll

Favourite movie
Dora

Name
Charlie

Age
5

If my name wasn't Charlie I'd like to be called
Pablo

Siblings
Coco

When I grow up I want to be a
soccer player for Chelsea (London)

Best friends
Pablo, Phoenix, Zac and Marine

Favourite colour
red and black (Essendon colours!)

Favourite book
AFL skills

Best song
Rock 'n' Roll Star by Oasis

Favourite toy
a laser pen

Favourite movie
Jungle Book

Lou Lou & Stella

The Westlake girls already have swag, stacks of swag. Stella is so cool she could very well start her own label and Lou Lou, well you just know that Lou is going to be famous one day. The Westlake girls are ones to watch and their rooms are created by them, exclusively. Their mum, fashion stylist Nathalie, and their dad, fashion photographer Paul Westlake, have left the girls to do their rooms themselves. Stella and Lou Lou prove that style is something you are born with.

Name
Lou Lou

Age
8

If my name wasn't Lou Lou I'd like to be called
Saphire

When I grow up I want to be a
lead guitarist in a rock band and an Olympic runner!

Best friends
Izzy, Renee –Louise, Amelie and Romane

Favourite book
Fartiste

Best song
Dear Prudence by The Beatles

Favourite toy
pogo stick

Favourite movie
Despicable Me

Best thing about my room
my bed!

What do you sleep with at night?
Max, my teddy bear

L : "My favourite song is DEAR PRUDENCE by the beatles."

Name
Stella

Age
10

If my name wasn't Stella I'd like to be called
Ruby

Siblings
Lou Lou

Where in the family
first!

When I grow up I want to be an
actress

Favourite book
The Lost Island of Tamarind

Favourite movie
Harry Potter

Favourite toy
cosmetic science kit

S : "My favourite colour is PURPLE."

Cece (or Cecilia for long!) lives in New York City with her sister and parents. Her room errs on pretty with a painted mural and antique mirror while her downstairs playroom is the ultimate

Name
Cecilia

Age
7

If my name wasn't Cecilia I'd like to be called
Apple

When I grow up I want to be a
pet owner

Best friends
Jameira, Alexis, Lilly, Lucy, JJ, Brooke Alice and Beatrice

Favourite book
The Little Red Hen

Best song
You Are My Sunshine

Favourite toy
origami kit

Favourite movie
The Three Little Pigs (Disney)

Best thing about my room
the toys!

cleo & lucky

Rachel Castles' kids don't know what all the fuss is about their mum's label, Castle. The champion of fluoro and polka-dots, their rooms have never been anything but this bright. Personal love letters from their mum are embroidered and framed on their walls, along with paintings, framed medallions and other small victories. Whether their homes have been renovated or not, the Castle kids' rooms have always been full of art and colour. Rachel wouldn't have it any other way. "I love walking past them and no matter how messy they are, I leave the doors open so I can sneak a peek!" Filled walls make for a content mother. But how do you know when to stop, or even where to start? "I start with one piece, contrast the next in colour and literally don't stop till the room is at its fill!"

castle

C×

C : When I grow up I want to be a RSPCA Animal rescue person

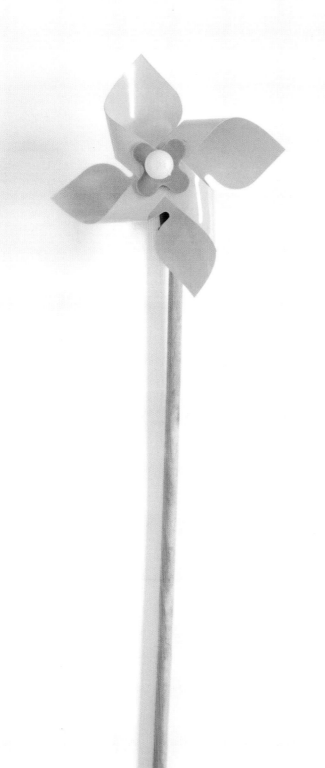

Name
Cleo

Age
10

My mum and dad are
Rachel and Daren

Siblings
brother

If my name wasn't Cleo I'd like to be called
Millie

Favourite colour
silver

Favourite book
The Curious Incident of the Dog in the Night-time

Best song
Grease songs

Best thing about my room
privacy

Favourite movie
Grease and Fame

What's your favourite song?

L: Michelle Jackson and black eyed pies

Name
Lucas (Lucky)

Age
7

If my name wan't Lucas I'd like to be called
Zac

Siblings
Cleopatra

When I grow up I want to be
like my dad

Favourite book
Toby Alone

Favourite toy
wolverine claws

Favourite movie
Dragonball

Best thing about my room
double bed

What do you sleep with at night?
my big f at broken arm

Jimmy and Audrey

Formerly the main living and dining spaces of the Federation home, these rooms are now his and her rooms for twins Audrey and Jimmy. The original bi-fold doors are left always pulled back so there is a distinct but almost invisible line between his and her space. Mantles in each room give them the opportunity to show their individuality and mother Nicole recommends letting the twins "create their own signature independent of one another". She should know, being a mother to five all up. The twins are her youngest and she sees them in this room set up for a long while to come. "It is ideal actually, they can shut the middle door in time to come, but for now it's a huge space where they happily retreat to for hours on end solo and with each other."

A : "My favourite book is Harry Potter (all of them)."

A : "The best thing about my room is it's big and has sliding doors to my brother."

J : "My favourite day of the week is Friday because I have ice cream
at the end of the day and I do lots of sport."

Name	Name
Audrey	Jimmy
Age	Age
8	8
Siblings	When I grow up I want to be a
Jimmy, Ava, Ruben and Esther	detective
Where in the family	Favourite book
equal last	Diary of a Wimpy Kid
When I grow up I want to be a	Best song
singer/vet	Hello by The Potbelleez
Best friends	Best friends
Anya, Luca and Jade	Ari, Fred and Charlie

J A S P E R

With antique traders as parents, Jasper's room is going to be the recipient of some interesting furniture. But nothing that's impractical. Decadently bohemian is the overriding style of the two-storey terrace, where there is a handsome library downstairs and Jasper and his brother's room upstairs. David and Nicole wanted the kids' rooms to share their love of English eccentric style and is a great case in point of going the whole house over with conviction, instead of watering down your own style when it comes to the kids' spaces.

Name
Jasper

My mum and dad are
David and Nicole

Age
5 and 3/4

If my name wasn't Jasper I'd like to be called
Benji

When I grow up I want to be a
fireman

Favourite day of the week
Friday (sport day at school)

Favourite colour
green

Favourite book
any book on dinosaurs

Best song
Bad by Michael Jackson

Favourite toy
lego

Favourite movie
Star Wars

What do you sleep with at night?
my green blankie

On the tag:

RPAH   1716891
PAGE, BABY OF NICOLE
DW–B   UBBNC   17/12/2009
Dr: LUDLOW,J   M   01:0
42 Juliett St

J : "The best thing about my room is I have a toy box underneath
my bed and my daddy painted stuff on my wall."

Max

Oh Max, you are a lucky boy. His graffittied chair says it all.

Name
Max

Age
15 months

My mum and dad are
mumma and dadda

If my name wasn't Max
I'd like to be called
I don't know, but I get called
'naughty baby' a lot

Favourite book
Pooh Bear

Favourite toy
Pooh Bear and my big car

Best song
my dad's 80s music

What do you sleep with at night?
Pooh Bear — I can't sleep
without him

pepa and hazel

Their mum is a talented fashion designer and their dad a mid-century furniture specialist. Art and a lot of found elements make these charming rooms cosy and well-loved within the context of a large architectural home. Modern spaces filled with bright eye candy, it is little wonder that these rooms are the prized spots in the house.

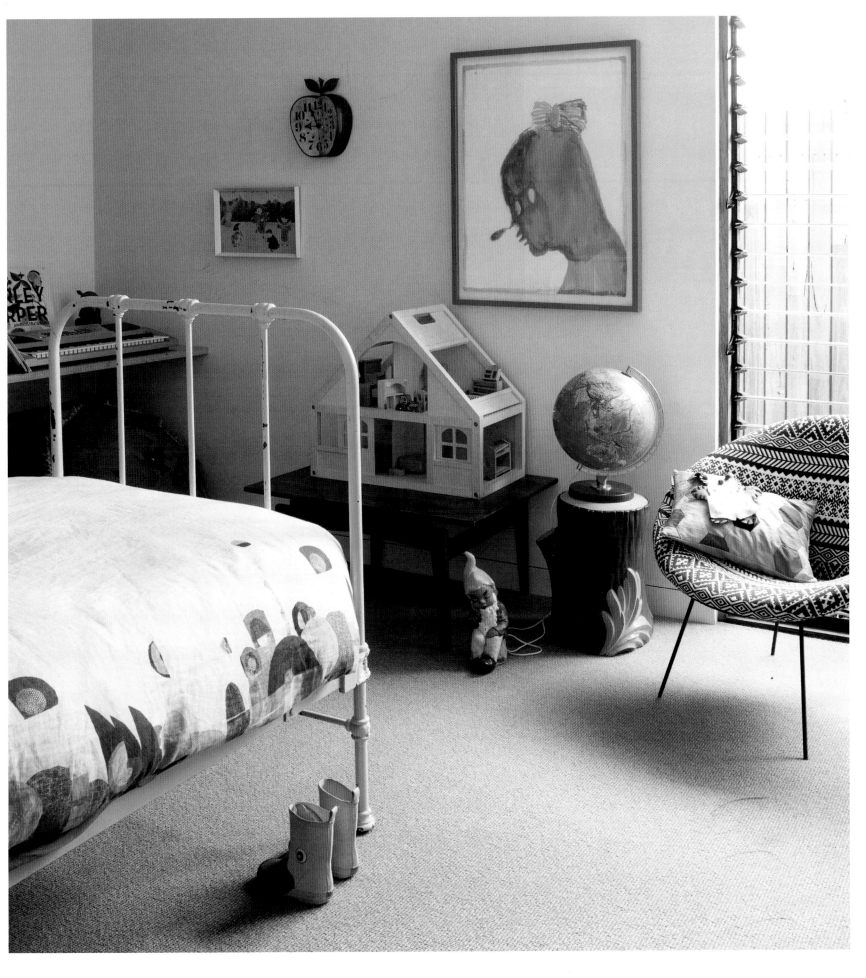

I : "The best thing about my room is my bed."

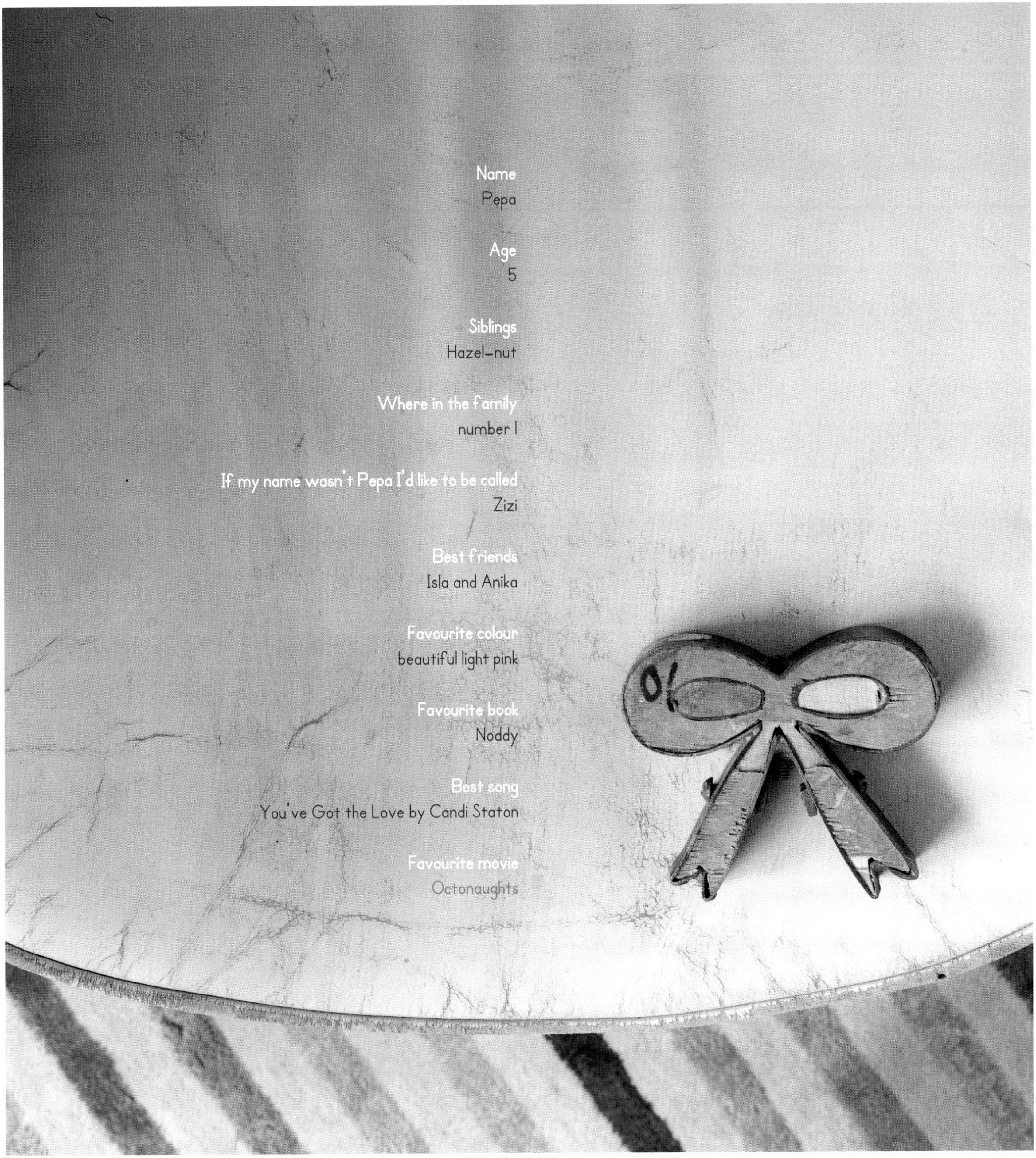

Name
Pepa

Age
5

Siblings
Hazel-nut

Where in the family
number 1

If my name wasn't Pepa I'd like to be called
Zizi

Best friends
Isla and Anika

Favourite colour
beautiful light pink

Favourite book
Noddy

Best song
You've Got the Love by Candi Staton

Favourite movie
Octonaughts

Name
Hazel Jane Angelucci

Age
2

If my name wasn't Hazel I'd like to be called
Cherry

When I grow up I want to be a
mummy

Best friends
pa, nanny, Eddie across the road

Favourite colour
dark sparkly pink

Best song
Mamma Mia

H : "My favourite book is Pooh Bear."

India

India has grown up living among mid-century furniture and collectables—her mother is a mid-century design academic. Her room mixes design collectables alongside Ken and Barbie with great success. India's room also demonstrates the beautiful energy of teak—the wood works beautifully with red, yellows and white.

Name
India

My mum and dad are
the best!

Age
8

Where in the family
eldest and mummy's princess

If my name wasn't India I'd like to be called
Aria

Favourite colour
sparkly gold and silver

Favourite book
Little Women

Best thing about my room
my bed—it was mummy's when she was little

What do you sleep with at night?
Britt Bear

holly,
baxter and bailey

Ivory, eggshell and touches of powdery pink with
ingenious storage units for the new twins—hooray
for big sister Holly Mae.

*

Name
Holly Mae

Age
just 4

Siblings
Bailey and Baxter

Where in the family
first

If my name wasn't Holly
I'd like to be called
Fairy Holly

Favourite day of the week
gymnastics day (Tuesday)

Best song
You've Got a Friend in Me from Toy Story

Best thing about my room
my secret cupboard (bedside table)

Favourite toy
'Favourite Holly' the bear

Favourite movie
Toy Story 3

H : "My favourite book is Pinkalicious."

Sunday

It's a standard story—on the weekdays architects and their families live in ultra modern spaces and then on the weekends, they revert to the simpler charms of more modest ones. Sunday lives a sliding-doors life on the weekends in her parent's cosy farmhouse. Her pea-green bunks that she shares with brother Roman are always filled with friends during sleepovers. The entire house is painted in the same colour—a sound way to give a house personality!

Name
Sunday

Age
8

If my name wasn't Sunday I'd like to be called
Tuesday

Where in the family
youngest but only girl

When I grow up I want to be a
vet

Favourite day of the week
Sunday of course!

Favourite book
Pippi Longstocking and Ramona Quimby books

Best song
Single Ladies by Beyoncé!

Favourite toy
american girl

Favourite movie
Marley & Me

Best thing about my room
I have a lot of space to spread out

Ty

The upper deck is a dedicated play area and the
lower deck is for beddy-byes. Nautical, but nice,
introducing Captain Ty!

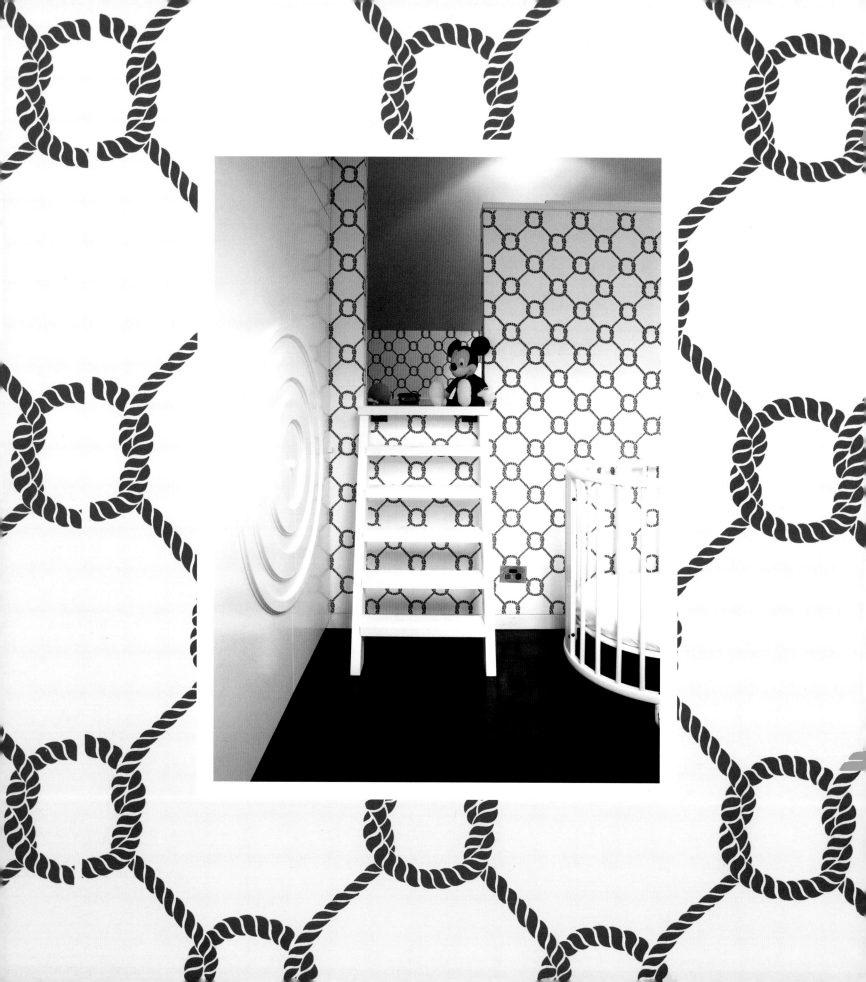

Name
Ty

Age
2 and 3/4

If my name wasn't Ty I'd like to be called
Boo

When I grow up I want to be a
fireman

Favourite day of the week
Friday (music class!)

Best friends
Gracie, Hazel, Finn, Tommy and Toby

Favourite colour
yellow

Favourite book
all of them!

Best song
Who's That Girl by Guy Sebastian

Favourite toy
guitar

T : "The best thing about my room is my play room!"

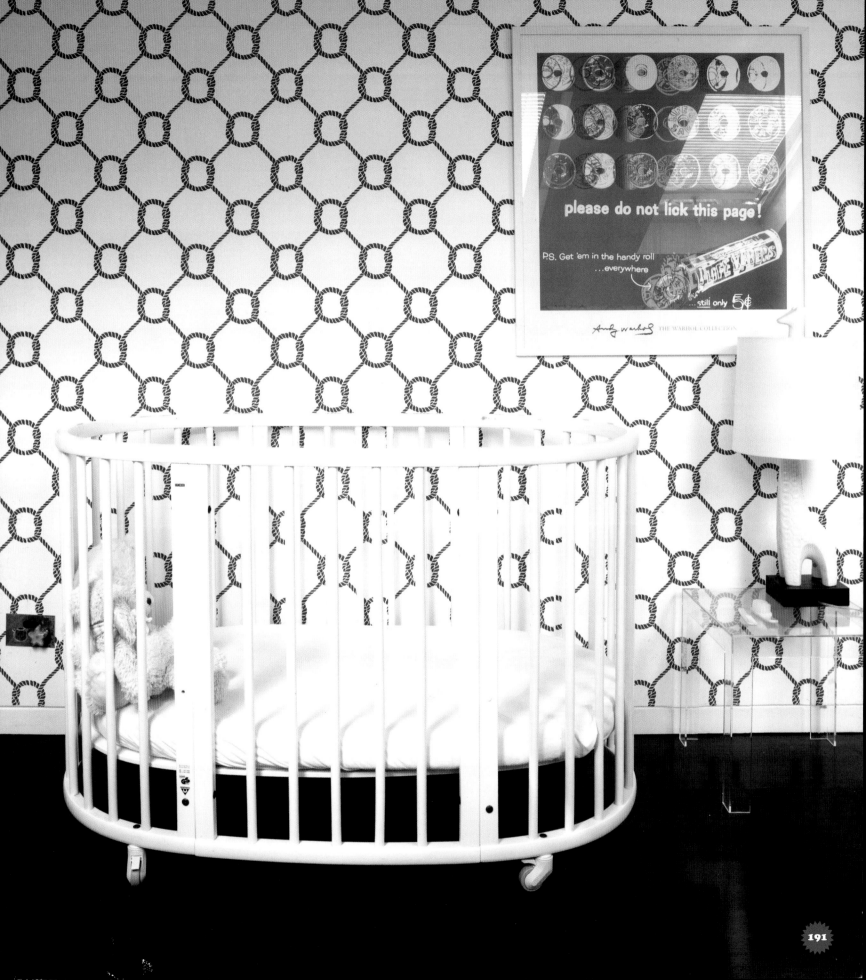

please do not lick this page !

P.S. Get 'em in the handy roll
...everywhere

...still only 5¢

Andy Warhol THE WARHOL COLLECTION

A third baby daughter rarely gets the pink room! So a charmed combination of mustard, red and white is chosen to compliment the dark floorboards. A host of hand-me-downs reflect Bea's easy-going nature. This colour combination is one to consider for shared rooms or a room that you'd like to be gender-neutral.

I like milk. A lot. I also like fun. A lot. I laugh always and despite my at-home haircuts, I still manage to look the cutest in my family. I am the youngest of three, but at least I am the boss of my dog August. He is my best friend. We sit and watch In The Night Garden together, but sometimes we like being together in my room when it's sunny. I have my own bed, but we all know I sleep with my mum and dad! —B

Oliver

Where to begin with a teenage boy's room? Here is your foolproof colour scheme right here! Teal does all the work, while a second hand, wall-mounted marlin takes care of the decorating. Sometimes the simplest remedies are the most succinct and successful. Oliver's room is a testament to this. Underdone can often be just-perfectly done when catering for this age group.

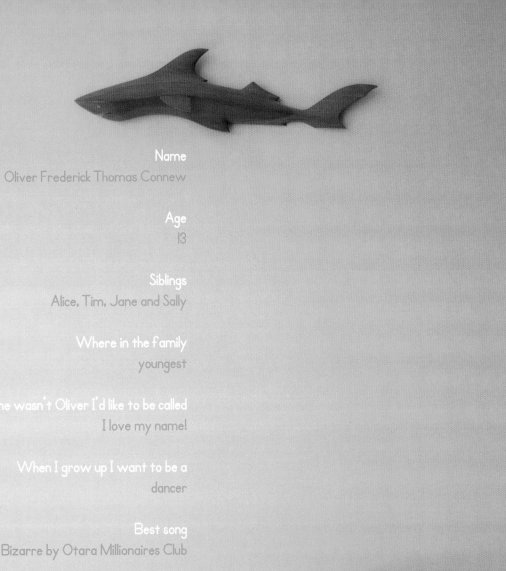

Name
Oliver Frederick Thomas Connew

Age
13

Siblings
Alice, Tim, Jane and Sally

Where in the family
youngest

If my name wasn't Oliver I'd like to be called
I love my name!

When I grow up I want to be a
dancer

Best song
How Bizarre by Otara Millionaires Club

Favourite colour
green

Favourite movie
Toy Story

THANK YOU

It's a big ask to open your house up, let alone your child's room. Possibly the biggest threat to the whole house. The purpose of this book is to show kids' spaces pretty much as they are, doors open, a super quick tidy and away we go. Any person who has children knows that this in itself is a gracious act so to all the parents, thank you.

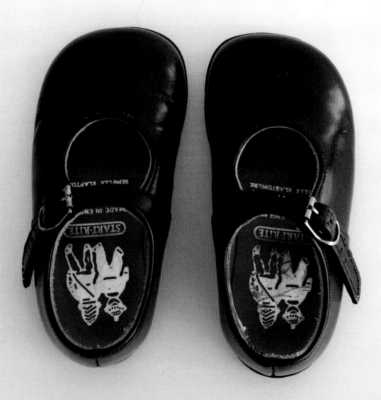

Camera-ready kids of all ages love photographer Jason Busch. That's probably because he is like a big kid. He tells jokes, laughs a lot, and never blows his lid. His mother is a kinder teacher and is super proud!

Graphic designer Penny's room was immaculate and so was her shiny bob. For such a girly girl, she had a thing for all things motorised and collected little cars. She is, just FYI, married to Jason and they make an unreal double act.

Growing up on a banana farm gave Megan Morton a love of yellow. While small people are the hardest to decorate for, they have proven to be some of her best clients! She is a mother of three, stylist and writer of two other books on interiors, Home Love and Things I Love. She has a place called The School where styling, art and making are taught to adults and children.

First published in Australia in 2013
by Thames & Hudson Australia Pty Ltd
11 Central Boulevard Portside Business Park
Port Melbourne Victoria 3207
ABN: 72 004 751 964

www.thameshudson.com.au

First Edition
16 15 14 13   5 4 3 2 1

ISBN: 978 050050 037 8

National Library of Australia
Cataloguing-in-Publication entry
Morton, Megan.
I love my room: children's rooms you and your children will
love / Megan Morton, Jason Busch, Penny Shek.
9780500500378 (hbk.)
Children's rooms.
Interior decoration.
Busch, Jason.
Shek, Penny.
747.77

Thanks to the generous font designers who have spent hours creating some of the fonts we have used in this book.

In order of appearance:
p1 Title: Primer Print by Larabie Fonts / p5 Subtitles: Print Clearly by BV Fonts / p5 Contents: Eager Naturalist by Tepid Monkey Fonts / Intros: Print Clearly by BV Fonts / Interviews: Primer Print by Larabie Fonts / p11 Betty Jean and Evie: Florencesans Outline by Apostrophic Labs / p16 Bridgette: Malache Crunch by Larabie Fonts / p28 Elodie: CrayonE by C. Verchery / p53 Millie and Sebastian: Fuchsiabuddha by Tracey Bleeden / p55 Jemima: National First Font Dotted by Roger White / p61 Tyke and Ari: Warren by Marian Fonts / p69 Eva: Primer Print / p73 Lana and Scarlet: Eager Naturalist by Tepid Monkey Fonts / p80 Ella and Marley: Chauncy Snowman by Chank Diesel / p87 April: Bric-a-Braque by Nick's Fonts / p94 Maddie and Cooper: Print Dashed by BV Fonts / p99 Nicholas and Sasha: Rechtman by David Rakowski / p110 Indigo and Chilli: Ballpark Weiner by Mickey Rossi / p117 Charlie and Coco: Caracteres L1 by Frank Rausch / p130 Loulou and Stella: Fuchsiabuddha by Tracey Bleeden / p139 Cleo and Lucky: Daryl Short by Daryl L. Houston / p164 Pepa and Hazel: Plum Bal by C. Verchery / p171 India: Creampuff by Nick's Fonts / p183 Sunday: Typewriterhand by Jon Grafton

Photography by Jason Busch.

Words by Megan Mortan and styling, except for Elodie (p28–33), Holly, Baxter, Bailey (p174–181) and Jemima's (p54–59) rooms where the styling is by Heidi Gill, and Jasper (p157) styling by Emma Cotterill.

Illustrations by Heidi Gill, except on Indigo and Chilli's pages where the drawings are by Louella Tuckey, and Millie and Sebastian's title drawn by Jemima Storch.

Editing by Stephanie Williams.

Design by Penny Shek.

Printed and bound in Singapore by Imago.